THE SEA
MY HEAD

Poetry and song

Laurence McPartlin

ISBN: 978-1-9996359-6-1

Also by Laurence McPartlin:

Wake the Stars (2019) Collingwood

for Beverley

To Mary

Thankyou for all
you Support,

Mac x

TABLE OF CONTENTS

ACKNOWLEDGMENTS

*"To see a World in a Grain of Sand
And a Heaven in a Wild Flower,
Hold Infinity in the palm of your hand
And Eternity in an hour."*
– William Blake

Thank you to my family and friends who have supported and encouraged me throughout. Once again, I owe a great gratitude to my good friend and editor, John Simes, who has taken my poetry to heart. Listening to him read out each one was endearing and profound. His patience and enthusiasm lifted me many times, but most of all his passion to make each one special.

Thanks to Rory McPartlin for typing up the initial draft and his advice on the format; without his help it would still be in long hand (my computer skills are still at the abacus stage).

Special thanks to Lisa Dyer for her skilful and artistic photography, for producing the cover and overlooking the overall layout. It's a joy to watch her work.

Many thanks to Mathew Holland for his painting of the Skylark sailing around Burgh Island.

Finally, I would like to thank John Eliot, dear friend and fellow poet, for all his support and for introducing some of my poetry to the international world. Also, thanks for his kind permission to use one of his pastel sketches (guitar art), Which I'm happy to say is still hanging on my wall.

Foreword

This is Laurence McPartlin at his most reflective and meditative. The joys and rhythms of folk and dance are still there to provide the momentum and energy that drive his words and thinking. In this deeply rewarding collection, Laurence is examining the individuals who have contributed something precious to his life and, through the prism of his family, he develops a buoyant and absorbing vision of the world.

There are ancient locations that trigger his memory and emotions - Burgh Island evokes the fisherman's songs and sea shanties that accompany the dazzling light from moon and stars; 'The Croft in Sutherland' draws forth the shifting ghosts of men and women and those who went to war never to return. These poems are full of voices, tongues that have been stilled by time are given breath and honour by Laurence's joyous verse and extraordinary eye for detail. But it is important that these voices are heard: 'through our eyes/The lives of others Speak,/Past and present come Together'.

> In Hangershell Rock
> There's a spirit
> Here,
> Raw boned and
> Primitive
>
> It lifts me up
> Blunts my breath,
> Shows me skies
> I can't forget.

In Laurence's poetry we have the remaking of modern life into a form that honours and re-energises the work of distant generations, and draws them into the present, to bring idealism and energy to our Covid-cursed world. In Guernica, the songs of fishermen are silent, stopped by the evil of mechanised war; but in St. Hilda's church, the sound of bells will drive the devil out. In Laurence's work, the life force always re-emerges.

In the exuberant, Away the Lads, it is the rough hands of working folk who shape the day. 'Where Neptune waits with his rusty fork, We'll tie his beard to the mast alright, and dip his tail in a barrel of rum, and let him whistle to the stars and sun.'

And finally, to his great love, his family and grandchildren: the tide is out, there is space to sing and play. 'Fill your buckets, laugh at the Sun, trawl your nets 'Till your arms are spun.'

This is a fine collection from Laurence; in its vision and completeness it echoes Wordsworth's pastoral vision and the Romantic poets' magic realism. But Laurence's voice is real and urgent, folks. Join the dance and listen.

John Simes

December 9, 2021, Challaborough, Devon, UK.

A Time of Childhood, Spent

Sometimes I sink
Under the weight
Of memories
Daisy mooned
And petal rimmed.

Chasing clouds
And laughing skies
To places I
Once played,
Lost in childhood games.

Rocks break,
shells crack, and
Flowers wait for
The curlew's shrill.

To wake the
Countryside from
Slumber,
Cradle deep in
A world of stars,
Calling out to me.

Time and space
Are everything,
For my sparrow song
To milk the light,
And spread my
Wings again.

Burgh Island (autumn)

The Pilchard Inn
Clings to the rocks
And the shining sea
Ebbs and flows
Below the mantle
Of her seaweed skirt.

Strips of sand become
Refuge for sea birds,
And the island
Reshuffles itself
To a slower pace.

Where lyrical lips
Rise to the chorus
Of fisherman's songs,
Roused by fire
And ale.

Time expands,
Entire days live
Longer
Whatever the hour
Day or night, and
Sounds slip across
The water,
Floating and drifting
On a windless swell.

Gathering shipwrecks
And shanties
Mussels and clams,
Highways of flotsam
And splashes of light
That dance on
Pearls
Drinking the moon.

(for Ben and Clare)

Of Dreams and Death

I have forgotten most
Of the hours,
Memories of sorrow
And joy
Collide and fade,
Like winter's hand
Wrenched from
A crow wind sky,
Exhausted with regret.

What I loved the
Most, no longer
Tells me of
The skinny kid
Of yesterday.

The desire to
Reach for
Wider skies
And never look back,
Conceals a life
That struggles to
Free itself
From the chains of
Dreams and death.

Like something stolen
Or hidden within,
It's hard to get
Close
When your heart
Fills your eyes
On unfound grief
That sucks the stone
And bleeds
The leaf.

Every Other Leaf

Sometimes, I feel
Vulnerable
Happy and sad
All at once,
Withdrawing into
A labyrinth of
Emotion where
Solemn thoughts
Overwhelm.

Time is a matter
Of fact,
It sings and flows
Without my help,
And everything appears
For what it is
Yet for me
To unlock what
Suffers most.

I must scuttle
The moon and
Resist every reflection
That bends my will,
And diverts me from
The truth and
Realise the void I'm in.

Blind to the scent,
of the blood root
Tongue,
Open
Every other leaf
That darkened my
Sun.

Peel the rind
And fly again.

The Croft (Sutherland)

It was abandoned
Years ago
When men went to war
And never returned,
The women folk just
Packed up
What they could
And moved away.

Evidence of how
They lived is everywhere,
A simple life a
Working life,
Now silently collapsing
In on itself with
The help of nature's hand.

Some photographs still
Hang from the walls,
A powerful conduit
Of reasons and dreams
That summon up a
Common thread
Invisible but real.

And through our eyes
The lives of others
Speak,
Past and present come
Together
And the spirit
Of stone opens the
Gates of memories, for
Us to trace in silence.

Looking back from
The hill
I thought of every
Thunderstorm and savage
Wind that will rot
The timbers and
Snap the rock, till
All that's left
Are ashes
Open to the sky.

Spring

The good earth
Opens its mouth
And drinks from
The rain filled
Sky,
Swelling seeds
And roots,
Cracking winters jaw.

Every pulse beats
Faster,
Free from the
Breath of frost
That hung its
Coat on bone-white
Rock,
Filled every
Crack and throat.

Soon the primrose
And the crocus
Will flame the
Woodland purse.

And leave no doubt
For the moonstruck
Hare,
To slip its sleeve
And wax the
Lips of spring.

(for Lisa and Charlie Dyer)

Cassandre's Dream

Cassandre is dreaming
Of Ronsard,
She sees her body
Entwined with his,
No longer captive to
A sulking moon

But free to touch
Life's flame,
Her bird-like heart
Is singing,
Locked within loves cure.

The Loire slips by
Unnoticed
Lost to the sea and stars,
All that matters is
The truth,
A gift in time intended.

Where all the threads
Have come together,
Revealing a tapestry
Complete.

Café Ty Pierre (Roscoff)

The boatmen have arrived
And the stone piers are
Thick with activity,
Soon the café will be busy
And the smell of fresh
Coffee and croissants will
Bring promise to the day
And a world that speaks to me.

I love this place, it's
A painting unfinished
Still wet, waiting to be
Added to.
The rhythm of the harbour
Embraces you,
Transparent, sincere –
A conquest of harmony.

Voices old as bronze
Share stories with the
Young.
I understand what they're saying,
It's like pressed petals in a book
Of memories.
Coming back to life,
I could spend all day
Just listening.

Conscience

Every time
I come to the
Same conclusion.

It's lonely speaking
To your conscience,
It scrapes your
Heart and scratches
Your eyes,
Takes you on strange
Paths
Where everything
Collides.

And any destination
You had in mind
Is scuttled
From the start,
Completely tangled up
Quarrelling all the time.

The silence is deep
Gravity fed
Exhausting and extreme,
Till somehow you
Realise
It's hopeless
What you're trying
To achieve.

Just stroke the
Wings of weightless
Dreams,
Let the rumours in,
Be content
With a thirsty night
And ride
The dirty wind.

Catch you on a Flip Flop

Towns rot
People die
Act it out
Beat the pain
Suffer the moment.

The damage is done
Search for air
Hang on to life
Lick your wounds
Move on.

Survive the pains
Of love and hate
Weld the hinge
Fix the gate.

Hold on to
Flesh and purse
Passion first
Negotiate the fee
Lie and cheat
Suck the marrow
From the cleat.

Never use an
Honest word
Progress must
Be made
Rock the boat
Throw the dice
Go for
Overload.

Feed the need
Bang the drum
Kick the bucket
Sail away
Grab your flip flops
And a takeaway.

Thanks for popping in.

City Streets

Buildings of all
Descriptions sit
Side by side,
A madhouse of
Doors and windows
Living
Separate lives.

Everything is
On the move,
Loading and unloading
Morning and night,
A common scene
Of every day,
Sharp as
A butcher's knife.

Pavements are
Stacked with
The human stride,
The saddest eyes
I've ever seen,
Turning inwards
On the world,
Riding on
A slipstream.

It's a scarecrow,
Desolation of
Traffic and
Graveyard skin,
That blows and spills
A cinder coat
On everything.

And the Clean
Air Act is
Shoved around.

Under someone's
Dark and
Breathless ceiling.

Last Train Home

Midnight train
Fogged up brains,
Cold fish eyes staring
Into Space,
What thoughts they have
I can't say,
Every grain of sand
Has filled their heads,
Where light should play.

A man like me
Is always watching,
In case they need a
Priest.
I know they're breathing,
The smell of booze
And food slowly covers
Me, like concrete.

I suspect they've
Been to the city
Gone to see the sights,
Must have blown their minds
Poor things.
They're country boys alright,
Whoever organised this -
Should be shot,
For such a wicked thing.

Wicked

Hands clasped and
Hair crammed in
Hats,
It's the same
Every day
Winter or spring.

Beautiful women
Gather and thread
Through narrow streets,
Toward the church
For bells and Hallelujahs.

I have no wish
To follow them
Or clip their Angel wings,
The weight of flesh has
Raked my eyes,
Every trick and step.

I sat outside the cafe
Becalmed,
With my wine and cigarettes,
You can't go wrong
I said to myself,
Every mind must flourish.

So, let them
sing to gods and
Saints,
keep them safe
and well, I'll drink my wine
From the rattling vine
And smoke
The thighs of hell.

Hangershell Rock

The fire of
Life returns,
And the shoulders
Of Hangershell rock
Shrug off the
Morning mist.

Above me
Drifting in the
Light air,
A sparrow hawk
Breaks the spell
Of solitude.

And the sound
Of water, slipping
Through peaty vaults
And heather sprigs,
Sing away the
Silence.

There's a spirit
Here,
Raw boned and
Primitive, a
Living beauty
That rises and
Blows across the
Bracken blaze.

It lifts me up
Blunts my breath,
Shows me skies
I can't forget.

And when the
Drifting hills
Get tired of my
Feet,
I'll fold my dreams
And fall asleep.

(for Rory)

River Song

The voice of the
River

Unlocks tree and
Root,
A beautiful noise
Of paddle drums
And water flutes.

Fiddle spun and
Trumpet blown,
Smiling and shouting
At every lip of
Hedgerow,
Spinning shade and
Veins of
Sparkling light.

Where shoals of
Stars swim
Weightless,
Whistling in every
Wheel and yawn
Of her flow.

And when she
Breathes
Cello deep
Humming the sun
To sleep,
The sea is
Waiting to collect
Her,
Loud as brass and
Rhythm wrapped
Her journey is complete.

(for Catherine McPartlin)

The Blasket Fisherman

Time coughs,
Blowing sleep
And ghosts from
Dreams and bones.

Make ready the
Boat and stitch
The wounds of
Gaping nets,
Rimed with salt
And sweat.

The drums of
The sea are
Riddled with tricks,
The Blasket fisherman
Must keep his bleary
Eyes from sleep.

Every trough
And every swell
Will test his skill,
And curse his course.
Her womb is only
Death.

Blind to wood and
Sail where
Shoulders ache,
And bruised hands
Hold fast to every
Rope and stave.

Pity the poor
Fisherman who
Hunts the shapeless
Seas,
Keep him safe
From the knees
Of rocks.

And pray for him,
Till the curve of land
Comes singing.

Kathleen

The hillsides and meadows
Are awake
Filled with wild flowers
And song birds,
Stairways of lanterns
Rich in blossom.

How lovely it is
To hear the bees singing,
My feet are smiling
Happy to roam.

On days like this
My mother always
Comes to me,
Bright eyed and
Laughing like a mountain spring.

The sun is spinning
Strawberry light and
For a moment,
We are one.

Wish

I threw a penny
Into the moorland
Stream,
And made a wish.

I wished that all
Wars would end,
And peace would
Come at last.

If you're ever
Passing this way,
And life is still
The same.

Please search
For my
Penny dream.

And try again.

Sylvette and the Sculptor

The last rays
Of the sun
Gather strength,
A brief and
Urgent pulse
Of light,
Skin tight,
Silent.

Revealing the sculptor's
Hands,
Chisel sharp,
Locked in tight
In a dream world
Which will outlast
Memories and the
Grains of men.

The universe
Ignores him and
The mirror widens
To new dimensions
And depth, where
Every vein and
Sinew become
An island
To itself.

And the space
He holds in
His mind
Must not retrace
Or doubt,
Every blow and
Breath must set
Her beauty free.

So, she can speak
And watch the
Poets weep.

(for Dave Holland)

Love in the Haystack

The energy of
Love,
Wild love
Reaping the
Passion.

Kisses long,
Kisses deep.

Tasting sweat
And scented
Breath.

Flaming every
Heart wing
Spring.

'Till it bursts
And ripens
Every limb.

And leaves
The haystack
Smouldering.

Time

Small Pools of
Water,
Cold stone,
Sweating moon.

Life goes on
Without walls,
And the weeping
Heart
Shoulders the stable
Of dreams,
Where mountains fly
Beneath an unsown
Sky with a
Voice that laments
The breath of time.

Eager to reach out,
To love
And love again.

Beyond the sirens
Of a lifetime.

The Sea Is in My Head

The drama of solitude
I understand.

Inner contemplation
Is rare in this dark
Maze of the modern
World.

Sitting here,
Scratching away at
My old guitar,
Ascending from one
Successive note to
The next.

I'm no longer
Conscious of what
I'm playing.

Fears and moods
Remind me of how
Many times I've
Become someone else.

Eager to reveal
And transmit
The lies that keep
Me safe from

Worthless words and
Cruel knives,
That trespass
In my thoughts
When the sea is in my head.

Every Blip and Switch

Unplug the television
Lock your iphone
In some drawer,
Take a walk in
The countryside
And live a little more.

Let your eyes
Rake every tree
And rock
Forget your troubles
And woes.

Lay naked in a
Tiny stream and
Feel the water
Flow.

Make faces in
The clouds and
Watch the sun
Go down.

Look at the stars,
Tiny sparks
Just like you and me
Spinning in the universe
The way it's always been.

Who knows? You may
Start a conversation
Without a text
Or emoji smile,
And discover for yourself
What's outside.

Instead of being a
Slave
To every blip and switch
Drowning in the uploads
With all the little tricks.

Bob Dylan and Me

The record player
Is on,
Bob Dylan's in the
Groove
Spinning out
Mr Tambourine Man.

I'm thinking
About school,
Thinking about
Girls,
Thinking about
Writing poetry.

I've decided
To write one now
For the blonde
Girl down the
Street,
With the body of a
Princess and
Eyes that speak.

My desire
Your desire
Hearts on fire
Let's take it
To the wire.

Then Bob gets
All fired up
With
Lay Lady Lay,
At this point
I was smouldering,
Tangled up in blue.

So, I cancelled
School forever,
Threw my homework
In the bin,
And started singing
Along with Bob
The Times They are 'a Changing.

Skylark

Nothing is excessive
Aboard the skylark today.

The sharp relief of the
Island watches over her
And the soft swell
Under our eyes
Mirrors her shape.

In a few fleeting
Moments
The dimensions of
Water and sky are
Distilled,
Unbroken pure space
Seized by some
Invisible energy.

All the blues and
Greens are flowering,
One intense burst
Of colour and
Pristine light.

When days like this
Slip away,
Something in the heart,
Composed and profound,
Is utterly embedded.

Never to be abandoned,
Forever saved.

(for Matthew and Kate Holland)

The Skylark by Matthew Holland

Dartmoor

Winter's breath no
Longer lingers.
Her grip, that tempered
The moor in ice
And snow,
Has been carried away
By skylark and thrush.

Revealing a landscape
To rediscover and
Trespass where you will,
Or carve out a place
And watch the earth
Disappear,
Stretching out time.

Deep within granite
And fern
Another universe exists,
That invites you to
Look closer and,
Let your deepest
Thoughts drift.

Before your footsteps
Fade and give way
To heather and gorse.

Flowers in a Vase

The hours of
Flowers are
Lonely
Stuck inside
A vase.

All motion and
Colour bite the
Door of death,
Fading like
Weeping hearts
Gathering regrets
In a growing
Void of silence.

Till there are no
Kisses left.

Old Wounds

The afternoon has
Faded like a
Crumpled flower,
And the rusting
Moon has left
Her silver on
The shoreline.

With pieces of
Wood and washed
Up dreams,
Spilling open without
Reflection on the
Dreamless sand.

Old wounds have
Returned inside
My head like
A graveyard moaning,
Under the weight of
Voiceless stone
Laden with wine
And grief.

It's hard to trap
The floating seeds
When the
midnight wolf
Comes to feed,
Every petal is torn
'Till the burden of
Sleep sinks
Within these walls
And sets me free.

Of Rags and Prayers

Jack's coat folds
Around him,
Stained and tired.
The numerous bags
He carries are
Stuffed with relics,
Held together by
Bits of string
And hope.

All day he has
Walked up and down
The long narrow
Street, reciting
Poems and psalms.

The world slips by,
Reflection and shadow.
A glass sea that
Knows nothing of
His seashell heart,
That calls out from
Some deep memory.

And, when light
Fades and darkness
Finds him sleeping
On his broken raft
Of rags and prayers,
Blades of dreams
Come to him,
And drain his eyes
Of tears.

Over The Hills Not Far Away

I have no cross
To bare,
My heart beats
And breaths a
Love of life
And wanderlust.

Time becomes a
Matter of fact,
No need to hurry,
Nobody owns anything
Out here,
Everything around
Resonates in every
Sense,
Whatever season
Turned and spent.

Nothing sounds warm
It's something you
Must feel, and all
The struggles for
Happiness that you
Pursue are surely
The hardest.

That only represent
Themselves in the
Smallest way,
Wasted dense and
Full of torment.

I'm no longer
Suspicious or
Unfaithful when
Exhaustion turns
To sleep, I've
Practiced all the
Distances and
My eyes have
Learned to see.

Poet

Hook and bone,
He mutters,
Hook and bone.
I've had a belly
Full of tides
And broken ropes,
Maggot bread and
Sailor's woes.

I've written all
I can
To satisfy their
Salty throats,
From lullabies
To roaring odes.

I will struggle
No more
With broken dreams
And
Lame wing doubts.

I will return
To the summer
Grass,
And watch stars
Fall like fires,
Flowers of the
Night,

And let them
Wash my threadbare
Coat,
Till all the sea
Is out.

Lorca

Rustling leaves
Olive trees,
Jasmine and oleander,
Betrayed
By lemon sharp tongues
Hungry for death.

The moon is crying,
Ashamed to look at
The stars,
Gypsies gather up
Water droplets in silence,
The wild rose is dead.

Sentenced to death
By men in black capes,
Who never hear the nightingale
Or understand the
World of fireflies.

The song of life
Has been silenced;
Lost to a sea
Of sunsets where
Sunflowers grieve
And tiny fishes hide
In shadow,
Never to speak again.

Guitar art by John Eliot

Guitar

Guitar,
Mistress of all
Feeds,
The sea and stars
Tracks the moon to
Punish and bruise
Sucks the rhythms
From my fingers that
Beat with pain and
Curse the flames
That bleed and
Beg for more.

(to John Eliot – dear friend and poet)

Fields of Eden

Blonde wheat,
Wind in our
Hair.

Powder blue
Sky,
Birds on the
Wing.

For you my
Love
I've come to
Sing

Hold me to
Your
Apron breast.

And dance me
Through the
Fields of Eden.

(For Beverley)

Be my Scissor String

I love you
Blonde gypsy spear,
Do not wait for
Me to trespass.

In the blue
Afternoon,
Let the yellow
Sun
Copper your breasts
And lark your voice.

Hold me like a
Mandolin,
Be my scissor string.

Tie your ribbons
To my waist,
And listen to
Our hearts sing.

Laurie Lee

I am a stranger
Free to travel
Through your lands,
Plucked like a guitar,
Bursting with song.

I am both the sun and moon
At every moment.

My world is filled
With watery light and
Rainbows,
Where skies rise like
Fountains,
Gathering the sun's
Yellow,
Watching over me.

Over hills and
Down lanes where
Meadows sleep with
Wildflowers,
My heart beats like a
Ship on the sea.

The treasures of the day
I gather up
To share with you.

Before your dreams
Turn to lanterns,
And fly away.

Nerja

A colourful waterfall
Of language fills the
Narrow streets,
Its market day and
Everyone talks at once
Unable to press silence
To their lips.

Cosseted and expected
The rituals of customs
Endured for centuries,
Are a spectacle magnified
Exquisitely dressed and
Addictive.

Women with shawls
Of lace slip by
Carrying geraniums
For the weeping virgin
And tortured Christ,
Compassion and suffering
Expressed to perfection.

Thyme scented doorways
And cool courtyards
Invite you to sit
And watch the world
Go by,
Coffee strong and
Pastry sweet.

All sense of time
Is consumed in
A single luscious
Moment,
Seductive, raw and
Fluent,
A thousand kisses deep.

Plaza De- Toro's

Blood red sand
Yellow sun,
The bull is dead
It's over

Old moon
New day,
The way of life
Continues

That's all there
Is to it-
Everybody knows

The bull is dead
Blood red sand,
Yellow sun,
It is over.

Heart of Memory

In the heart of memory
Everything slows down,
Shadows stretch out
And shivers of light
Disappear through sleeping
Keyholes,
Where souls whisper
Like feathers in
A starless sky.

You remember the
Roads you travelled,
Kisses you left
Behind,
The shell cracked, grief,
And the fable ships,
You slipped aboard
And said goodbye.

Only to return
To clocks and bells,
Where day and night
Carry the weight of
Lamentation,
And you experience
The profound loneliness
Of the deathless void
That cannot speak.

Slave to the Sea

I am a slave
To the sea,
A peasant to
The sea,
Chained to all
Her moods,
And shipwreck
Thighs.

Deaf to the
Bells of the
Watery depths,
Blind to the
Whiplash tides.

And when she
Blows with
Curls and crowns,
To snap the boon
And strip the shrouds,
I'll chew the rime
And spit the comb.

On every plume
And snout,
Till all the
Stars dance
On her blouse!

And squeeze the
Billows out.

Balzac

Balzac shot the
Moon last night
And closed the
Gates,
A tear for his
Soul, a flower
For his grave.

In the half
Light, the shy
Shadow of his
Mother stands
By the cold stone
That mirrors
Her silence.

She remembers his
Eyes the most,
They outshone
Any flame or
Suffering saint
That sometimes
Surfaced in his
Dreams.

On the talking
Streets,
A wind full of
Stories and poems
 Born overnight from
 Ink-stained hands,
 Are shared like
 Songs filled with
 Stars and daylight
 Skies.

Ruins and Dust

The streets are
A thousand years old,
Washed by time
Bruised by storms,
The grand waste of
Cultures.

Scaled down and
Defused where
Life reflects no more
On faces, that
Call out to saints.

The brief eternity
In which they lived
Is locked in the
Spirit of stone, and
No one has a key
To lead them back.

No matter what
Miseries or
Stories they exchanged,
Mortalities last breath
Transcends to new
Dimensions.

And all that's left
Are a few gargoyles
That look down
With grim lips,
That smirk and curse
On ruins and dust,
Hanging on
To the last deceit.

Redemption

The raven's beak
Is in deep,
And the spoon
Moon is busy
Digging graves.

If the stars
Were a little
Closer I would
Ask for help but.

Blood is spilt
And wars go on,
The colour of
Day is darkness
Squeezed by time
Anvil cold.

And winters shroud
Just won't let go
Till the dove returns,
And the moon is
Free of the ravens
Grip
Whose only purpose is
To kill.

War

Ghosts slip through
The trees, silver
Threads from sombre
Beds calling mother.

All is lost on this
Shameless battlefield,
Riddled with
Cruel silence, gathering
Up the wreckage of
The day.

Pity my eyes for
What they have seen.
Give me something
For the pain.

I want to be a little
Bird and fly away, to
Somewhere I can sleep -
But the war goes on.

Gathering fields
Of seeds,
Blood on flesh, earth
On fire -
I cannot speak of love.

All around me
Savage graves and
Sorry rags
Turn my legs to waves,
Over and over again.

I taste tears and dust -
Wishing it would end.

Guernica

Songs of fisherman
Are silent,
Precious years and
Dreams, what could have been,
Murdered.

The sun is weeping,
Death has come to Guernica.

Bare hands search the
Rubble,
Hearts of faith, blood on stone.
The morning stars are
Bleeding,
On a landscape drowned in shadow.

This is a place
Wreathed in ruin and dust,
The kingdom of light
Receives no quarter.

On the hillside
A silver crucifix hangs
From the olive tree,
Consumed with grief
The dove has died.

Ruins (Rievaulx Abbey)

The last rays
Of the sun
Reveal a silhouette
Of ruptured stone,
Open to the sky.

Where shadows move,
Like damp fog,
Wavelike,
Circling the
Flaking walls.

Voices that once
Called out to saints
Have long vanished,
Sentenced to the
Belly of the wind
And frozen stars.

The energy of life
Is brief,
Daylight's door
Turns the key
To silence.

The infinite
Passage of time
Is complete.

St Hilda's Church

Time has milked
Her shell of
Stone,
Summer washed,
Winter groomed.

She stands like a
Rusty nail,
Gathering the
Rising sun around
Her fragile waist.

All burden and
Favour have paused
For breath,
The only sound
Comes from the sea
Whispers of
Eternal motion,
Gently folding
On the shoreline.

Soon voices will
Circle and resonate
Around the headland
Snout,
And the flower of

Their lives
Will sound her bells
Along the tidal walls,
And drive the
Devil out.

(for Stephen McPartlin)

Away the Lads

Away the lads
Bang the drum
Let's drink our
Ale to the
Stars and sun.

We'll test our
Skills on a broken
Tide,
Curse the devil
And spit in his eye.

Let's sail our
Boat where the
Water chokes the
Narrow river flute,
And ride the
Humpbacked wave
Toward the open sea.

Where Neptune waits
With his rusty fork,
And fishy tail
To prod our keel
And clip our sail.

Away the lads
Hold on tight,
We'll tie his beard
To the mast alright,
And dip his tail
In a barrel of rum,
And let him whistle
To the stars and sun.

Tide's Out

Fishing boats lay
Idle,
Keeled over on
The beach,
Barnacled and
Snoring out in
The midday heat.

And not a sound
Comes from the
Riverside, where
All the mussels sleep.

Seagulls swoop
And cockles poop,
And crusty crabs
Hide beneath
Small rocks and
Seaweed slip.

That trip bare
Feet
And scratch
Bare hands, when
Searching for shrimp
And juicy clams.

A feast to be had
When the tide is
Half mast,
Stranding tiny fishes
In pools of glass.

So, fill your buckets,
Laugh at the
Sun,
Trawl your nets
'Till your arms
Are spun,
Then brush the
Sand off your
Knees
And RUN!
The tide's coming in.

(for Erin and Libby)

Pale White Shore

Summer days are
Fine this year,
A young girl
Passes by,
She rests by
Swirling pools
Where the river
Meets the tide.

And to her side
Draws down the
Moon,
Blows a kiss
To the starry
Sky,
She's in love,
She's in love,
You can see
It in her eyes.

Come dance with me
On a pale white
Shore,
To the sound of the
Crazy sea,
Where wild winds take
Your breath away,
And set your spirit free.

Now the beaches
Are deserted,
There's nothing to
Declare,
A pocket full of
Sand
A memory here and there.

Oceans call out
To her
All dressed in
Blue and green,
The stars have
Found their magic
And the moon
Has touched a queen.

Come dance with me on......

(for Beverley)

About the Author

Laurence McPartlin was born in Hartlepool; after leaving school he worked in the local steelworks, before venturing to a new career at a hotel at Lochinver, Scotland. His travels then took him south to work in hotel management in Harrogate, before finally putting his roots down in the leafy South Hams, Devon, United Kingdom. He enjoys playing the guitar, song writing and sketching.

"You are all welcome to....

Come dance with me
On a pale white shore
To the sound of the crazy sea
Where wild winds take your breath away
And set your spirit free...."

You can find out more about Laurence at Collingwood Publishing and Media www.johnsimes.co.uk or contact him at: macduck52@icloud.com

More great books from Collingwood Publishing

by John Simes

The Dream Factory Trilogy:

The Dream Factory (2017), Matador
A Game of Chess (2018), Collingwood
Cape Farewell (2023), Collingwood

Short stories

The Upperthong Thunderbolt (2021), Collingwood

by Mary McClarey

Long Road, Many Turnings. (Paperback and e book)
Time for a Change (Paperback and ebook)
Another Mother's Child (Paperback and e book)
My Trip by Billy (e book)
Blink flash fiction second prizewinner included in the Fish 2020
Anthology

by Laurence McPartlin

Wake the Stars (2019) Collingwood
The Sea is in my Head (2022) Collingwood

**For more information contact: The Ivybridge Bookshop or
email me@johnsimes.co.uk**

Wake the Stars – Reader Reactions

A lovely collection of forty poems. Laurence McPartlin has created an anthology full of emotion and rhythm which transports the reader to another world. A great read and one which I enjoy dipping into every now and again ...and again.

Mary McClarey, Author

Wow! Wow! Wow! Wow! What poetry! The first copy of your book, Wake the Stars, arrived. Such accessible, beautiful stories, musical and sweet rhythm. I enjoyed every poem. The book is well done, high quality, well-edited. I love John Simes' foreword - short and precise. You must visit us Hope one day you come and read your poems to our students - probably during the Kistrech International poetry festival here   see you Laurence. Thanks a million times for this gem.

Dr. Christopher Okemwa
Founder Kistrech International Poetry Festival

It is telling from this collection that the poet is a writer of songs. These poems are lyrical, crafted pieces. Laurence holds a mirror for the reader that reflects not himself, nor the reader but the world as it is, not as the poet or reader expects it to be. In a carefully structured phrases from this collection, Wake the Stars, carefully edited and thought out, Laurence takes us to spaces unique that are beyond our usual experience. But these are not fantasy, this is his world told as storyteller in a very new and original way. Classic poetry and deserving of a wide audience.

John Eliot, Poet